Florence Bramford R.V.M. (Royal Victorian Medal)
1891–1985

Against a backdrop of British history, *From Cottage to Palace* presents the life of Florence Bramford, who became a Ladies' Maid to the Ladies in Waiting of *two* Queen Elizabeths, from 1939 to 1974.

This is the life of my great aunt Flo, as related mainly by herself through my aunt, Margaret Bramford. Great Aunt Flo had a Victorian childhood and an Edwardian adolescence. She was privileged to reside in many a royal residence with her Ladies in Waiting and was frequently invited to serve on Royal Tours all over the world. Her efficiency, enthusiasm, and good humour were much appreciated by all who knew her.

Richard Lyntton (Né Richard Bramford)
Philadelphia, 2022

From
COTTAGE
to
PALACE

BONUS

Margaret Bramford

**A Malchik Media &
richardlynttonbooks Publication**

Published by
Malchik Media & richardlynttonbooks

Copyright © 2023 Richard C.G. Lyntton

ISBN-13: 978-1-959755-03-6

Production by Gary A. Rosenberg • www.thebookcouple.com

About the cover image:

The Royal tour signed group photograph on the front cover features Florence Bramford (circled) with King George VI, Queen Elizabeth I, Princess Elizabeth (Queen Elizabeth II), and Princess Margaret on H.M.S. *Vanguard* en route to South Africa in 1947.

Click HERE or visit for the Worcestershire and Malvern History Series including *From Cottage to Palace*:

https://www.amazon.com/gp/product/ B09XC28GGL?ref_=dbs_p_mng_rwt_ser_ shvlr&storeType=ebooks

Click HERE or visit for *From Cottage to Palace* audiobook:

https://www.audible.com/pd/From- Cottage-to-Palace-Audiobook/ B0B3PQTSGZ

A Preview of
From Cottage to Palace

· ·

"George! George! Come quickly! Bang the dustbin lid! The bees are swarming!", shouted seven-year-old Florence, wearing a long white pinafore and sturdy buttoned boots.

It was noon on a Saturday in May 1898. Florence was running down the straight path of the long Worcestershire garden and banging together a saucepan and its lid. This was called "tanging" the bees.

Her brother George, nine years old, dark-haired, attired in his everyday knickerbocker suit and boots, soon followed her, making a commendable din. He looked like a mediaeval knight of Newbridge Green, striking his shield, the dustbin lid, with a stout stick.

The children's noisy duty on this fine May morning, in a hamlet close to Upton upon Severn, was to make their father's swarming bees settle in his garden, rather than in the field or orchard. A more experienced bee-keeper down the lane would then come to put the swarm back in the hive.

Florence and her brother were brought up on honey. Their father had three hives. Their mother sold honey. Before the end of May, a lady called Miss Anderson from The Glebe, would make her regular visit to their cottage and ask, "Have you any virgin honey?" By this, she meant early, pale honey.

"Good! They've settled on our apple tree," exclaimed George. "Dad will be pleased," remarked Florence, quietly. Their duty done, the girl and her brother looked fleetingly towards the blue Malvern hills in the distance. This was their favourite view.

1

Then they ran back to the house, past the long orderly rows of well-tended vegetables, the pink blossom of the apple trees and along the brick paths, lined by low, well-trimmed box hedges, which exuded a spicy aroma after summer rain.

Florence went back to the cottage kitchen to scrub the new potatoes for dinner. George ran down the lane to tell the bee-keeper about their swarm, before returning to the stay behind the cottage, where he was "cleaning out the pig".

Florence, named after her maternal grandmother, was the eldest daughter of George Bramford, who originated from the village of Laxton in Nottinghamshire, a truly mediaeval village. There, even today, they still operate the Open Field system, whereby the farmers cultivate strips of ground in different parts of the village.

Son of a Laxton farmer, and born in 1862, George Bramford had been recommended by the Reverend Henry Martin of Laxton, as "a promising young man", to be coachman to Colonel Sir Charles Johnson of The Hill, Upton upon Severn, in Worcestershire.

Lady Johnson, one of the Martin family of Ham Court, close to Upton, was a relative of this Laxton Rector. Servants, in those days, were often hired purely on the recommendation of relatives and friends.

"The Reverend Henry Martin had high standards," so George Bramford used to relate. "If he saw a flyspeck on his carriage window as he set off to visit a lady, he would ask his coachman to return home to have the window cleaned first. He was a good Vicar at Laxton. He was there for forty years. The poorer villagers would be given soup and blankets from the Rectory."

Thus, young George Bramford from Laxton came south to Upton upon Severn and remained in the service of the Johnson family for the rest of his working life. With his upright, spare figure, clean-cut features, alert and steady gaze, George became a capable and reliable coachman.

He looked smart in his navy blue livery, with white breeches for special occasions. The coachmen of each big house in the district could be identified by their distinctive livery the colours of their uniform. For Ham Court, it was green with red collars. The livery of Madresfield Court was red and black, while at Pull Court, Bushley, it was fawn.

Florence reminisced:

"Dad would drive the spring cart into Upton almost daily for groceries for The Hill. In the afternoons, he would drive his master and mistress to call on friends the Cherrys at Henwick, the Isaacs, or to catch a train at Upton station.

"On some days he might be driving a passenger or a parcel to one of the big houses nearby—The Hyde or The Boynes. Otherwise, he would be grooming the horses, cleaning the stables, the coach and the harness a never-ending job."

Florence would see her father sometimes, riding one horse and leading another, as he exercised them down Southend Lane, opposite his cottage, or took them to the blacksmith at Longden Heath. He would return home at the end of the day, smelling of horses and polished leather and still wearing his leather gaiters and strong boots.

"Best of all, George and I were allowed to ride in a cart with Dad, on special occasions. I remember how we would meet a train at Christmas and collect parcels of food for the Home of the Good Shepherd at Welland. My father's Lady Johnson was Patron of this Home. We children, wrapped in travelling rugs, would accompany Dad in the open cart, along the Hanley Road and back through Welland."

Soon after young George Bramford had arrived at The Hill, there had appeared a young lady, neat and lively, with dark hair and twinkling dark brown eyes. Eva Alice Wills had come to be lady's maid to Lady Johnson's sisters who also lived at The Hill—Miss

Ranira and Miss Jemima Martin, whose family home was Ham Court.

The young coachman from Nottinghamshire began noticing Eva as she went about her duties, for she would have to warn him when to be ready with her ladies' carriage. Her sparkle and decisive manner were an attraction to the calm, responsible young man with the serious face.

Eva's father, John Wills, also had twinkling dark brown eyes above his beard. He had been Station Master at Bradnich, Devon, where Eva was born in 1864, and then Station Master at Crediton. He was next appointed as Chief Clerk at the Harbour of the flourishing port of Bridgewater, Somerset.

Eva Alice often talked about her father's Bridgewater office, and his tall desk with a hefty ledger on it. "Looking outside, I would see the harbour alive with sailing ships, each with their brightly painted figureheads." The Harbour Master's house can still be seen near Bridgewater harbour.

The courtship at The Hill went well. George and Eva had their engagement photos taken by Norman May of Malvern. Eva Alice wears a velvet bustled dress, a brooch and a locket, looking roguish and a trifle vain. George wears a cutaway coat and waistcoat with covered buttons and a gold horseshoe tie pin. He gazes equably on the world.

They were married in St. Mary's Church, Bridgewater, on the 4th of June 1888. Their wedding photo, in the studio of H. Davey of Exeter, shows George in new pinstriped trousers, waistcoat hiding a fob watch, jacket with bound edges, winged collar and spotted silk tie. He is seated on a cushioned chair, upholstered in plush, with long cord fringes, beside a potted palm. From his direct gaze and firm mouth there flowed confidence and trust.

His wife stands at his elbow, her hands resting on his forearm, showing her engagement and wedding rings. She wears a dark dress, beaded with jet and has an ample ruched bustle. Her hair is swept up; she wears tiny earrings and a brooch. From her "Spanish" face, with full lips, her prominent eyes look soulful and a little apprehensive.

They were to set up home in a brick cottage with oak beams on the Ham Court estate. Their cottage had once been a "one up, one down", with stairs leading directly from the front door. In the 1870's the cottage had housed a Dame school, kept by old Mrs. Cowley for the local children. As a young man, George Bramford had been her lodger.

* * *

The Bramford's ancient cottage is still very much in existence. Brick-faced in the eighteenth century, it has a half-timbered inner structure, which may well be Elizabethan or Jacobean. The oak beams, hand-cut, still retain small pieces of bark. The elm floor of the oldest bedroom is likely to have been used originally as timbers of a ship.

The plaster on the interior walls was recently found to contain horsehair, proclaiming its age.

The cottage is marked on a map dated 1701, looking like "a little shed". The Drum and Monkey Inn, next door, is not marked on that map, showing it is less old.

"The annual rent," said Florence, "which my father paid in 1890 was £6.14s and there was a pigsty in the back yard. Everyone kept a pig in those days and lived off the salted sides of bacon for months. I well remember the bacon and the chine (the backbone) being hung on hooks in the kitchen."

And now, one hundred years later, the cottage proudly bears the name BRAMFORD COTTAGE because the Bramford family had lived there for 93 years continuously. . . .

FINALE

Florence, whose mother was born in Devon, recited this to her nieces on her last birthday, when she was 94 years old:

> I be close on ninety-seven
> Born and bred in good old Devon.
> There's not a place in all the world
> That can compare with Devon.
>
> The Cornish seas be far and wide
> But the Devon seas be wider.
> And if you'll live as old as I
> Take Devon cream and cider.

❖ ❖ ❖

Florence Bramford:
A Life in Photos

#1. Signed (King George VI, Queen Elizabeth [Queen Consort], Princess Elizabeth, Princess Margaret) group photograph of The Royal Family and their staff on board HMS Vanguard *en route to their tour of South Africa, 1947.*

Close-up of Florence (circled)

The Royal Family and their staff on board HMS Vanguard en route to their tour of South Africa 1947

Margaret Bramford's handwritten note on the back of the signed photo.

#2. Royal Victorian Medal. Presented to Florence Bramford on HMY Britannia *on February 3, 1966 (coincidentally two days after the birthday of her great nephew—this book's publisher). This was the first time the Queen gave this particular order on* Britannia.

Close-up of the Royal Victorian Medal.

"So I had to go to the Queen one evening, after my supper and before her dinner. She was in her sitting room and she presented my medal to me. And the doctor, who always used to travel with us, Admiral Sir Derek Steele-Perkins, he received an order as well."

"I met the Admiral next morning and he said, 'Oh, Miss Bramford, I want to congratulate you. You've made history. The Queen has never given that order on Britannia before, so it has gone down in the Log Book.' "

(*From Cottage to Palace,* page 82)

*#3. Brooch given to Florence Bramford by Queen
Elizabeth II after global Royal Tour in 1954.*

#4. Denmark

#5. Nigeria 1956

#6. Iran (Persia then)

#7. Belgium

#8. South Africa

#9. France

#10. Germany

#11. Unknown (Probably Finland or Sweden)

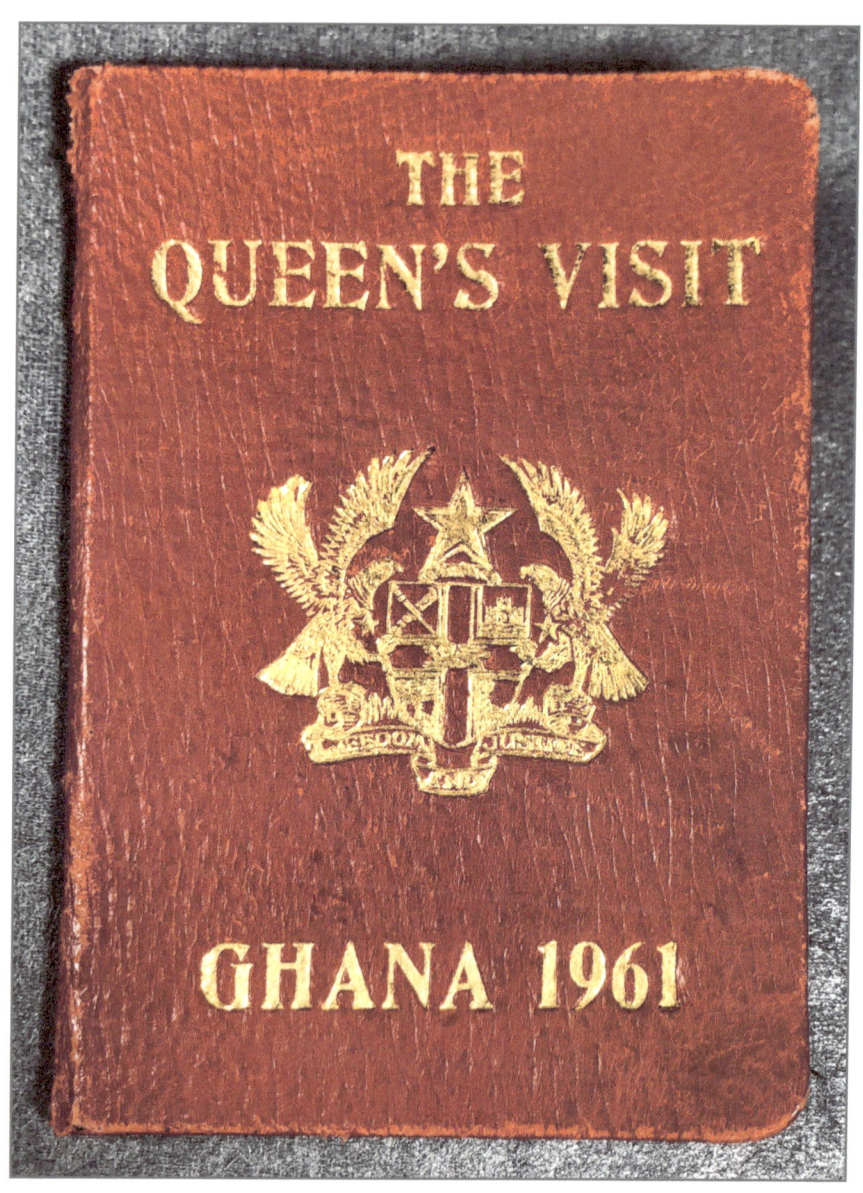

#12. The Queen's Visit Ghana 1961

The Ghana Police (Special Pass) No........**27**

THE QUEENS VISIT 1961

Bearer *Miss F.* *BRAMFORD*

Maid to Lady-In-Waiting

residing at *Accra*

is authorised to enter or leave *Christiansborg Castle*

and Residencies

via *Main Entrance* at *Any Time* by day and night

or the purpose of *Official* *Duties*

during the period *9/11/61* to *20/11/61*

Signature of Holder and Stamp   Commissioner of Police, Ghana

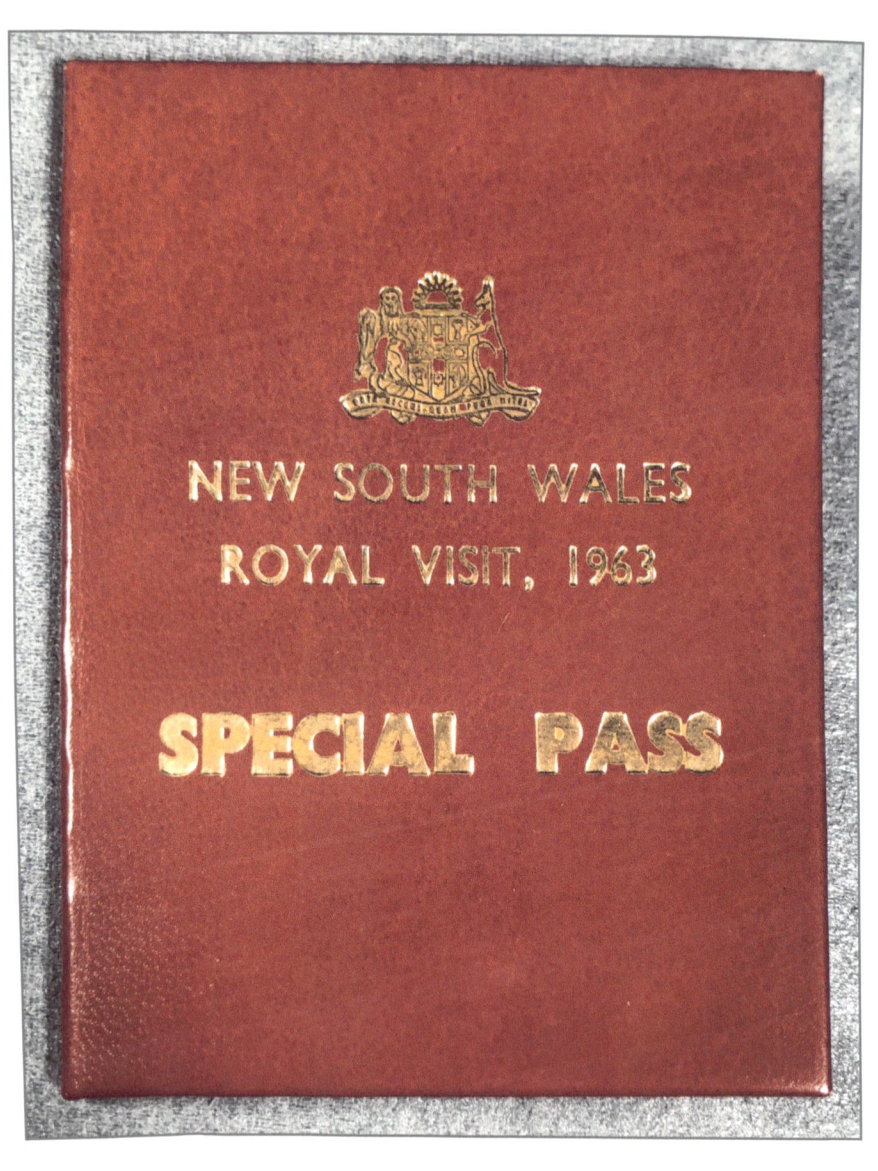

#13. New South Wales Royal Visit 1963

No. 27

Name _Miss F. Bramford_

Position _Maid_

G.M. Gray
State Director

THE BEARER
of this Pass has the
right to enter
any Enclosure or Function
including
Government House
and the Sydney Cove Terminal

•

The Police and all officials will
kindly facilitate her movements
in every possible manner

43788 1.63 V. C. N. BLIGHT, GOVERNMENT PRINTER

#14. Jamaica 1963

This is to certify that the
bearer is <u>Miss F. Bramford</u>

<u>F B ram ford</u>

a member of the Royal Party.

~~He~~/She is to be given every

possible assistance during

~~his~~/her stay in Jamaica.

Commissioner of Police
22.3.66.

#15. Australia 1963

#16. Western Australia 1963

**Click HERE or visit for the Worcestershire
and Malvern History Series including**
From Cottage to Palace:

https://www.amazon.com/gp/product/
B09XC28GGL?ref_=dbs_p_mng_rwt_ser_
shvlr&storeType=ebooks

Click HERE or visit for
From Cottage to Palace **audiobook:**

https://www.audible.com/pd/From-
Cottage-to-Palace-Audiobook/
B0B3PQTSGZ

www.ingramcontent.com/pod-product-compliance
Ingram Content Group UK Ltd.
Pitfield, Milton Keynes, MK11 3LW, UK
UKHW051453050225

4462UKWH00018B/63